D1228463

ALL AROUND THE WORLD
ZIMBABWE

by Kristine Spanier

pogo

Ideas for Parents and Teachers

Pogo Books let children practice reading informational text while introducing them to nonfiction features such as headings, labels, sidebars, maps, and diagrams, as well as a table of contents, glossary, and index.

Carefully leveled text with a strong photo match offers early fluent readers the support they need to succeed.

Before Reading

- "Walk" through the book and point out the various nonfiction features. Ask the student what purpose each feature serves.
- Look at the glossary together. Read and discuss the words.

Read the Book

- Have the child read the book independently.
- Invite him or her to list questions that arise from reading.

After Reading

- Discuss the child's questions. Talk about how he or she might find answers to those questions.
- Prompt the child to think more. Ask: Zimbabwe is landlocked. Where do you live? It is landlocked?

Pogo Books are published by Jump!
5357 Penn Avenue South
Minneapolis, MN 55419
www.jumplibrary.com

Copyright © 2020 Jump!
International copyright reserved in all countries.
No part of this book may be reproduced in any form without written permission from the publisher.

Library of Congress Cataloging-in-Publication Data

Names: Spanier, Kristine, author.
Title: Zimbabwe / by Kristine Spanier.
Description: Minneapolis, Minnesota : Jump!, Inc., 2020.
Series: All around the world | Audience: Ages 7-10.
Identifiers: LCCN 2018052233 (print)
LCCN 2018053918 (ebook)
ISBN 9781641286732 (ebook)
ISBN 9781641286718 (hardcover : alk. paper)
ISBN 9781641286725 (pbk.)
Subjects: LCSH: Zimbabwe—Juvenile literature.
Zimbabwe—Social life and customs—Juvenile literature.
Classification: LCC DT2889 (ebook)
LCC DT2889 .S63 2020 (print) | DDC 968.91—dc23
LC record available at https://lccn.loc.gov/2018052233

Editor: Susanne Bushman
Designer: Molly Ballanger

Photo Credits: maiteali/iStock, cover; Lucian Coman/Shutterstock, 1; Pixfiction/Shutterstock, 3; Sopotnicki/Shutterstock, 4; Maximiliane Wagner/Shutterstock, 5; evenfh/Shutterstock, 6-7; Tom Cockrem/Getty, 8-9; Yury Birukov/Shutterstock, 10; jez_bennett/iStock, 11; Pawel Gaul/iStock, 12-13; Howard Klaaste/Shutterstock, 14t; Utopia_88/iStock, 14b; Vladimir Wrangel/Shutterstock, 14-15t; Papa Bravo/Shutterstock, 14-15b; Maks Narodenko/Shutterstock, 16l; Soru Epotok/Shutterstock, 16m; panuwat panyacharoen/Shutterstock, 16r; Kevspic/Dreamstime, 17; CECIL BO DZWOWA/Shutterstock, 18-19; Robert Muckley/Getty, 20-21; Shutterstock, 23; iStock, 23.

Printed in the United States of America at Corporate Graphics in North Mankato, Minnesota.

TABLE OF CONTENTS

CHAPTER 1

WELCOME TO ZIMBABWE!

Would you like to spot a lion? Or try sadza? It is ground corn porridge. Eat it with green vegetables and fish.

sadza ·····▶

Listen to the roaring Victoria Falls. In late winter, this is one of the world's largest waterfalls! Welcome to Zimbabwe!

Victoria Falls

Great Zimbabwe is in the southeast. It is made up of **ruins** from an **ancient** city. People lived and worked here from around 1000 to 1450 CE. How do we know? **Artifacts** have been found here. Glass beads. Porcelain. Gold.

DID YOU KNOW?

The ruins in Great Zimbabwe gave Zimbabwe its name. It means "stone houses." The country used to be called Rhodesia.

Great
Zimbabwe

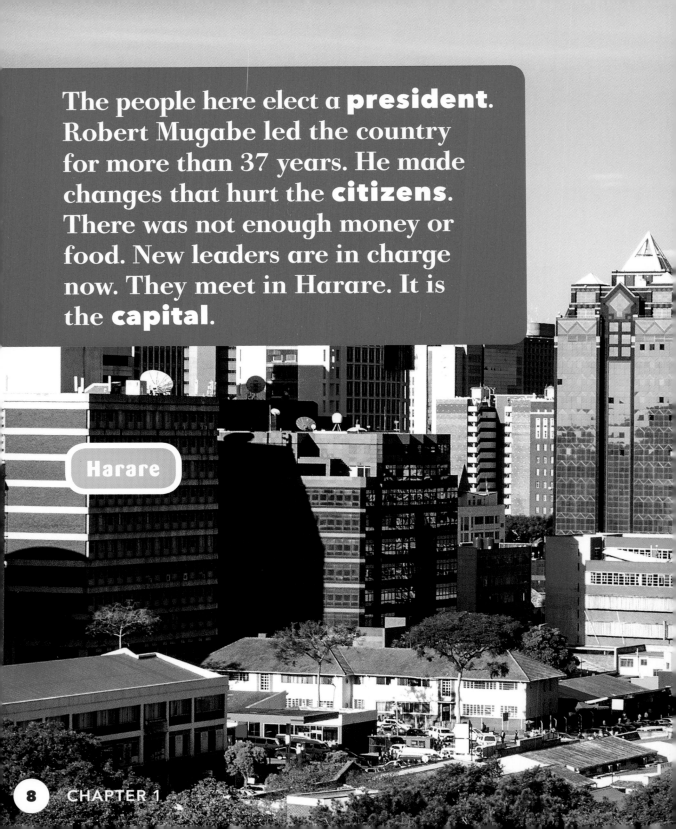

The people here elect a **president**. Robert Mugabe led the country for more than 37 years. He made changes that hurt the **citizens**. There was not enough money or food. New leaders are in charge now. They meet in Harare. It is the **capital**.

Harare

TAKE A LOOK!

Zimbabwe's flag is important to its citizens. What do the different parts **symbolize**?

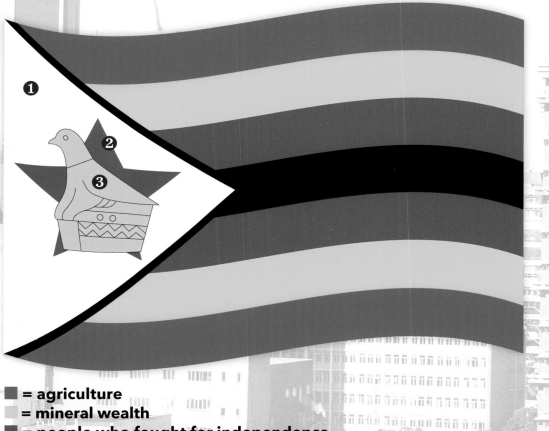

■ = agriculture
■ = mineral wealth
■ = people who fought for independence
■ = native people

❶ white triangle: peace
❷ red star: cooperation with other nations
❸ golden bird: long history

CHAPTER 2

LAND AND ANIMALS

Can large boulders balance on smaller rocks? Yes! These **formations** are found all over Zimbabwe. They are known as kopjes.

kopjes ·····▶

This country is **landlocked**. Mana Pools National Park is in the north. Many animals live here. Birds stop here while they **migrate**.

Mana Pools
National Park

Many rivers are in this country. The Zambezi River creates the border with Zambia. The Limpopo River is south.

The Great Dyke is a line of rock ridges and hills. It runs through the center of the country. It is rich with **minerals**.

WHAT DO YOU THINK?

Minerals make up one third of the country's **exports**. What minerals are found here? Chromium. Nickel. Platinum. What **natural resources** are found where you live?

Zambezi River

Victoria Falls

serval

ratel

chacma

impala

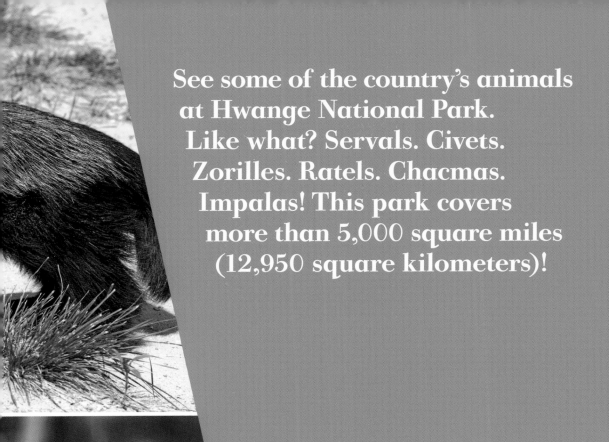

See some of the country's animals
at Hwange National Park.
Like what? Servals. Civets.
Zorilles. Ratels. Chacmas.
Impalas! This park covers
more than 5,000 square miles
(12,950 square kilometers)!

CHAPTER 3

LIFE IN ZIMBABWE

More than half of the workers here farm. What **crops** do they grow? Corn. Wheat. Barley. Soybeans. Bananas. Oranges. Some raise cattle.

corn

soybean

barley

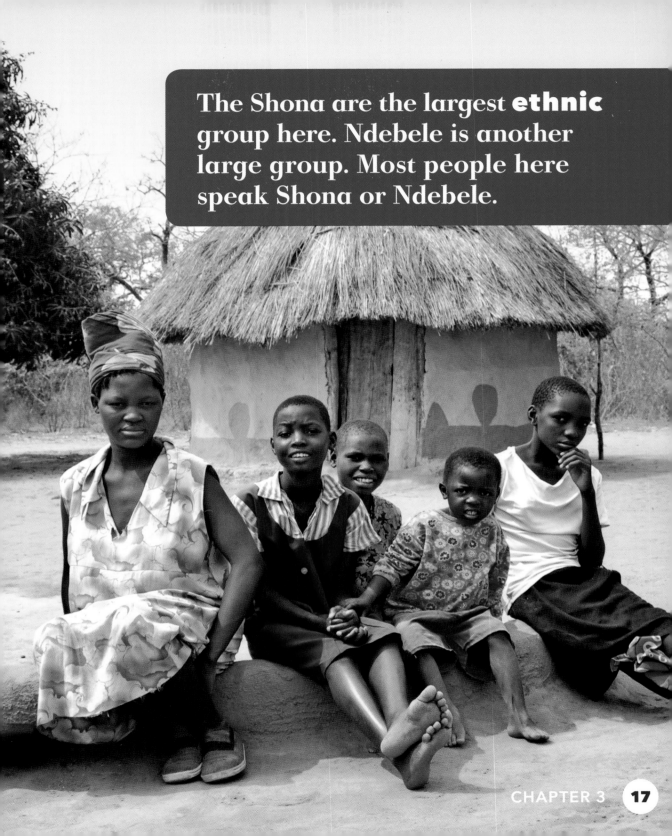

The Shona are the largest **ethnic** group here. Ndebele is another large group. Most people here speak Shona or Ndebele.

Most kids here start school when they are seven years old. They try to attend for at least seven years. Families must pay for school fees. Not all families can afford this. Classes are taught in English. This is a challenge for students who speak different languages.

WHAT DO YOU THINK?

Students here attend school year-round! They have three school terms. Each is three months long. There are one-month breaks between terms. Would you like to attend school year-round?

Soccer is the most popular sport here. People also play basketball. Or netball. This is like basketball. They might play cricket or rugby, too.

Dance is an important **tradition** for people here. So is art. People make beautiful pottery and sculptures.

Zimbabwe has a long history. Would you like to visit?

QUICK FACTS & TOOLS

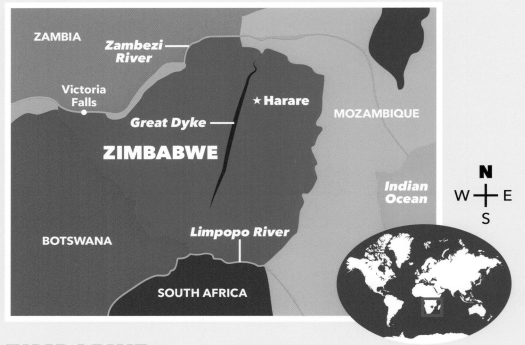

ZIMBABWE

Location: southern Africa

Size: 150,872 square miles (390,757 square kilometers)

Population: 14,030,368 (July 2018 estimate)

Capital: Harare

Type of Government: semi-presidential republic

Languages: Shona, Ndebele, English, 13 minority languages

Exports: platinum, cotton, gold, textiles, clothing

Currency: various currencies used

GLOSSARY

ancient: Very old.

artifacts: Objects made by human beings in the past.

capital: A city where government leaders meet.

citizens: People who have full rights in a certain country, such as the right to work and the right to vote.

crops: Plants grown for food.

ethnic: Of or having to do with a group of people sharing the same national origins, language, or culture.

exports: Products sold to different countries.

formations: Structures or arrangements of something.

landlocked: Not having any borders that touch the sea.

migrate: To move from one region or habitat to another.

minerals: Naturally occurring substances obtained from the ground, usually for humans to use.

natural resources: Materials produced by Earth that are necessary or useful to people.

president: The leader of a country.

ruins: The remains of something that has collapsed or been destroyed.

symbolize: To represent a concept or an idea.

tradition: A custom, idea, or belief that is handed down from one generation to the next.

Zimbabwe's currencies

INDEX

TO LEARN MORE

Finding more information is as easy as 1, 2, 3.

1. Go to www.factsurfer.com
2. Enter "Zimbabwe" into the search box.
3. Click the "Surf" button to see a list of websites.

FACT SURFER